D0307038

PETER KENT'S
BIG BOOK OF
ARMOUR

KINGFISHER

First published 2010 by Kingfisher
an imprint of Macmillan Children's Books
a division of Macmillan Publishers Limited
20 New Wharf Road, London N1 9RR
Basingstoke and Oxford
Associated companies throughout the world
www.panmacmillan.com

Illustrations by: Peter Kent

ISBN 978-0-7534-1884-0

9 8 7 6 5 4 3 2 1
1TR/0410/WKT/UNT/157MA/C

A CIP catalogue record for this book
is available from the British Library.

Printed in China

Picture credit: p6–7 Shutterstock/mehmetsait

Contents

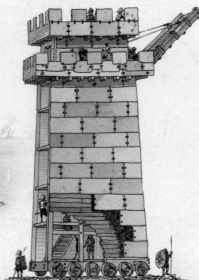

INTRODUCTION

When most people think of armour they imagine a clanking suit, the kind of clothing worn by a man whose tailor is a blacksmith, but there is more to it than that. Armour is defensive covering, something that protects the wearer from harm but not just in war. There are many more dangers to people than battleaxes, bullets and bombs. Most people put on some sort of armour every day, whether it's a bicycle helmet, shin pads or safety goggles. And it's not only people that wear it – just look at a tortoise, or the aptly named armadillo. Whenever something needs protection, there you'll find armour. From a battleship to a beetle, there's nothing like armour to keep it safe.

Strong plastic knee and elbow pads with a helmet keep this scooter-rider safe. They were unknown 30 years ago when grazed knees were universal.

Legs are in danger in a game of football with all those boots hacking at the ball. Pads save shins from cuts and bruises.

The shining knight in a polished suit on his equally well-protected horse is most people's idea of what armour looks like.

DIY can be lethal, too. Safety requires a pair of ear defenders, safety goggles and a dust mask.

The kitchen can be a dangerous place. An apron and oven gloves protect the cook from spitting fat and hot trays.

Strange concrete objects such as this are part of the sea coast's armour, defending it against the waves.

Soldiers long dreamed of armoured vehicles to keep them safe on the battlefield. This armoured war cart was used by Hussites from Bohemia in the 15th century.

Building sites can be almost as dangerous as battlefields, so builders wear helmets and steel-capped boots.

A helmet with a visor to protect his eyes against a toxic spray is standard wear for today's security guard.

Factor 50 sun cream acts as invisible armour, filtering out the harmful ultraviolet rays in sunlight.

Animals have worn armour long before there were humans. The hard plates covering an armadillo protect it against teeth and claws.

Even plants have armour. This spiny, outer layer covers the shiny, hard conker inside.

Insects live inside a complete suit of armour as they have their skeleton on the outside. The hard outer casing is, for their size, very strong.

EARTH'S ARMOUR

The atmosphere is an envelope of gases that surrounds the Earth – without it, no life would be possible. As the Earth moves through space, the atmosphere acts both as a shield, giving protection from most of the deadly rays and meteorites that continually bombard us, and container, stopping the air from escaping into space.

The atmosphere, which is about 700km thick, does not work like a normal sheet of armour – lumps of rock do not simply bounce off. A solid object piercing the atmosphere creates friction as its surface drags through the air, and more speed means more friction and more heat. Meteorites either burn up entirely, or only small fragments reach the ground. Only the very biggest meteor or asteroid could pass through the atmosphere in one large piece. The atmosphere also acts as a filter to radiation, only letting through sunlight, heat and some less harmful rays.

The exosphere is the very top layer. It starts at about 650km above the Earth and finally merges into space at about 8,000km.

Solar shield

Most meteorites burn up in the mesosphere at about 60–80km above Earth, where the air is thick enough to cause friction.

Although it is made of nothing but gas, the atmosphere is immensely heavy, weighing about 5,000 million million tonnes.

A spaceship descending to Earth begins to notice the effects of the atmosphere at about 120km above the surface. Without heat-resistant surfaces it would burn up.

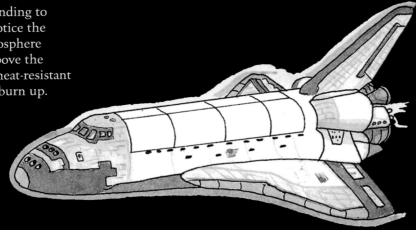

At about 85km above Earth, the ionosphere absorbs much of the ultraviolet light. Cosmic rays and gamma rays are also neutralized here.

One way of coping with global warming would be to create artificial solar shields to reflect the sun's rays back into space, rather like a windscreen shield that stops the inside of a car getting too hot.

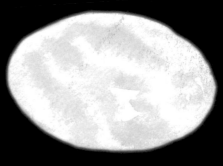

Solar shield

The vital part of the stratosphere is the ozone layer, at about 15–35km above Earth. This filters out ultraviolet light.

The lowest layer of the atmosphere is the troposphere. About 80 per cent of all the gases in the atmosphere are in this layer. This is where oxygen is thickest, and where the final filtering of harmful rays takes place.

COASTAL DEFENCE

When you are walking on a beach or scrambling up cliffs, you are playing on the gigantic suit of armour protecting the land in its everlasting battle with the sea. There are natural defences against the waves: hard, such as cliffs, and soft, such as sand dunes, but still the coast is washed away. Ever since people began to live by the sea they have been defending their homes and harbours against the waves. The Romans were the first to build built breakwaters, but it was the Dutch who started building sea defences on a large scale. For the Netherlands and other countries that lie below sea level, their sea defences are vital armour.

Gabions are a way of making large rocks by scooping up smaller ones and packing them in boxes made of wire mesh.

This sea wall has a slope at the bottom to make the waves break and a curved top to deflect the force back.

Wooden revetments are easily damaged by waves and need constant repair. They are unpopular because they stop people getting to the water.

CONCRETE BLOCKS

Interlocking concrete shapes make a great sea defence. These are made to many different designs but the most common is the 'dolos'. The legs lock together so they form an immovable barrier, while the spaces in between allow the water to wash through and lose most of its energy.

Xbloc

Accropod

Tetrapod

A-jack

Dolos

Akmon

200CE The great harbour of Ostia was the main port for Rome. The outer harbour with its curved breakwaters and lighthouse created a safe place to anchor.

9

ANIMAL ARMOUR

Millions of years before there were human designers of armour, nature had evolved the basic ways of providing bodily protection, for nearly every animal has an enemy that wants to kill it. The animal without any defence is soon extinct. The best defence is to run away or hide but for those who can't, nature has provided armour in the form of shells, scales and thick skins. The more dangerous an animal's enemies are, the more complete its armour has to be.

HORNS

The basic forms of weapons are clubs that crush, spears that stab and swords that cut. The horns of animals are the equivalent of spears.

Rhinoceros

Moose

Narwhal

TEETH

Animals' teeth are designed to cut and tear. The terrible fangs of Tyrannosaurus rex and the tiger's huge canines are the classic weapons of the predator.

Tiger

Crocodile

Tyrannosaurus rex

NATURAL ARMOUR

The strongest form of armour is a shell. Its continuous surface can resist heavy blows but it is heavy and restricts movement. The most flexible form of armour is a strong hide like that of an elephant or a hippopotamus, but to be effective it must be very thick.

Turtle

Cone shell

Conch shell

Ladybird

Elephant

Hippopotamus

A coat of bony plates or scales is easier to move in. It is strong but there are weak places in the joints.

Pangolin

Ankylosaurus

CLAWS

The paw of a grizzly bear is like a spiked club. The crab's claws and the golden eagle's talons are used to crush and grip their prey.

Bear

Crab

Golden eagle

BEAKS

Birds' beaks have many uses: the macaw's cracks open nuts; the woodpecker's chisels wood; the heron's spears fish; and the vulture's tears its prey.

Macaw

Woodpecker

Vulture

Heron

PLANT ARMOUR

Most of the world's creatures are vegetarians and, in order to survive, plants have evolved ways to protect themselves. Trees need a hard, outer layer to protect the growing wood inside and seeds need a case to protect them long enough for them to ripen. But the defences cannot be too good. Plants need to be eaten – if their armour was completely effective, animals would be unable to feed and would starve.

Bark protects the tree against cold, keeps in moisture, keeps out insects and prevents injury. It is continually renewed from within as the inner bark dies.

The seeds of the Bhutan pine are inside this cone made of woody plates.

The bark of the cork tree can be over a metre thick. It is mainly harvested to provide the corks for wine bottles.

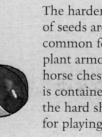

The hardened cases of seeds are the most common form of plant armour. The horse chestnut seed is contained within the hard shell used for playing conkers.

The cone of the maritime pine is made of woody scales reinforced with sharp prickles.

As coconut trees are very tall, their seedcases need to be very strong to avoid breaking when hitting the ground.

PRIMITIVE PROTECTION

20,000 BCE All basic armour must defend against stabbing and blows to the head.

The first pieces of armour were made from natural materials: shields were formed from woven twigs, wood or animal hide. Body armour used the natural toughness of skins and hide. Other primitive armour was made from hoops of wood, strips of bark, slats of wood or bone sewn into fabric, and rope woven into a stiff suit. Some shields and helmets were made from tortoise shells. All these 'green' forms of armour were no longer used as soon as metal was easily available.

1850

1780

 1890 CE The first armour was probably like this Dayak armour from Borneo, made of goat hides.

This Inuit wears a breastplate of walrus ivory plates laced together with rawhide.

1800 On the South Pacific Islands, strong armour was fashioned from coconut fibre rope and woven cane.

Wood bent into hoops and covered in hide made armour for Chukchi warriors from Siberia.

1400 The Aztecs wore very effective armour of padded linen. Knights wore suits to make them look like jaguars or eagles.

12

ANCIENT ARMOUR

It was in Egypt, the Middle East and China that civilization in cities and states first appeared. Quarrels between them led to fighting on a large scale, with properly organized armies, but it was the discovery of metal – first copper, then bronze and finally iron – that truly revolutionized warfare. Metal weapons cut with deadly efficiency, so more protection was necessary. The first armour was made of leather and thick cloth, sometimes reinforced with small metal plates.

1275 BCE Only the Egyptian pharaoh could afford a coat of bronze plates sewn on leather; soldiers wore armour of thick leather, hippopotamus hide or padded linen.

1020 BCE The Bible says that the giant Philistine, Goliath, wore armour of brass, but it was more likely to have been bronze.

3000 BCE The first Egyptian soldiers fought savage tribes armed only with primitive weapons. They did not need to wear armour and carried only large cowhide shields.

900 BCE These strange decorated bronze helmets were worn more for show than for serious fighting.

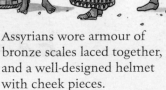

750 BCE Assyrians wore armour of bronze scales laced together, and a well-designed helmet with cheek pieces.

1300 BCE The Hittites were the first to use iron swords and helmets.

2500 BCE Sumerians wore long, thick leather cloaks strengthened with bronze discs in the same way as their wooden shields. Their helmets were made of leather or copper.

13

CLASSICAL ARMOUR

The most beautiful and elegant armour was made by the ancient Greeks, as you might expect from the people who built the Parthenon. Armour was so important to them they even had a god, Hephaistos, dedicated to metal working. A few centuries later, Rome was the greatest power in the western world. The Roman empire, stretching from the Arabian desert to the far north of Britain, was defended by a superb professional army.

1200 BCE At the siege of Troy warriors wore helmets made of boar tusks and carried huge cowhide shields.

1450 BCE Charioteers who didn't need to walk could wear heavy bronze suits made up of 15 individual pieces.

490 BCE Greek soldiers or hoplites wore bronze or leather body armour with bronze helmets and bronze greaves on their legs.

420 BCE Greek hoplites formed a solid mass called a phalanx. Each man was protected by a large shield and carried a long spear.

GREEK HELMETS

Greek helmets were beautifully shaped and skilfully made by hammering out a single sheet of bronze. Each city had its own distinctively shaped helmet.

Illyrian helmet

Spartan helmet

Corinthian helmet

Chalcidian helmet

Boeotian helmet

Thracian helmet

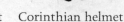

CELTIC WARRIORS

Most of the Romans' Celtic enemies wore no armour. Some even fought naked. No wonder the Romans nearly always won!

100CE Roman soldiers or legionaries wore a standardized armour of metal plates with a helmet that defended cheeks and neck. An apron of metal discs gave extra protection.

35CE Flexible plate armour was introduced in the reign of Tiberius. The plates were an effective defence but were light and easy to wear.

55BCE Legionaries in Caesar's time wore a chain-mail shirt and a bronze helmet. Officers wore a bronze cuirass which mimicked the muscles of the abdomen.

100CE The rectangular shields could be formed into a *testudo*, or tortoise, to make an instant and very effective 'tank'. It was used to attack walls and ramparts while under heavy bombardment.

MEDIEVAL ARMOUR

When the Roman Emperor was deposed in 456CE, Europe entered a period known as the Dark Ages. The continent splintered into a chaos of warring barbarian tribes. The peoples that replaced the Romans – the Saxons, Franks, Goths, Vandals and Lombards – were brave and fierce but very backward in military technology. They thought the Romans' armour made of metal plates was too complicated. The barbarian kings, nobles and warriors wore mail shirts and richly decorated helmets. Common soldiers had to make do with leather jerkins.

400CE

The Saxons were called after their saxes (long knives) and the Lombards after their long axes.

750

This noble is wearing a magnificent helmet decorated with gold. Most helmets of the Dark Ages are known as *spagenhelm*.

1120

The crusaders wore linen surcoats to protect them from the fierce heat. Their great battle helmets were very uncomfortable and very hard to see out of.

1400

Common soldiers wore leather jerkins called jacks. They were often strengthened with small plates of metal or horn. Their helmets were known as pots.

1400

Every knight needed a squire and a couple of servants to help him dress and to keep his armour clean.

1200

Suits of armour were still mainly made of mail, but plates of boiled leather were added to vulnerable parts.

1350

This is typical armour of the 100 Years War, with metal plates added to chain mail. The wasp waist look was very fashionable.

1500

A good horse was expensive and needed protection: a knight didn't want it to be killed under him or he would have to fight on foot.

800

The Vikings never wore helmets with horns. They did have ones that looked as if they were wearing spectacles, but the nose bar was more common.

1450

By the 1400s knights wore a suit completely made of plate armour, weighing about 35kg.

1066

The Normans wore mail shirts and helmets like the Vikings but added kite shields. These protected the legs as well as the body.

MAKING ARMOUR

Armourers were the most famous and best-paid medieval craftsmen in the Middle Ages. The best armour was made in Germany and Italy. Learning the skill of making complicated armour by hand took four years as an apprentice, and then another four as a paid workman. After passing an examination by making a special piece – his masterpiece – the workman became a master. Armourers combined to form a guild, which set prices and inspected work to make sure it was of the highest quality.

1 The master armourer took the order, measured the client and discussed what he wanted. Some clients left wax models of their limbs with their armourer, so he could make replacements without seeing them again.

2 A bar of wrought iron or soft steel was hammered flat, at first by a water-powered hammer and then by hand.

3 This reduced the bar to a thin sheet about 4mm thick.

4 The metal was cut into flat shapes with shears, following a pattern.

5 The parts were hammered into shape on a wooden mould. This was the most skilled part of the making process.

6 The parts were heated in a furnace to harden the surface. Every armourer had a secret recipe for this process. One smeared the surface of the metal with rancid pork lard, and wrapped it in goatskin covered in clay.

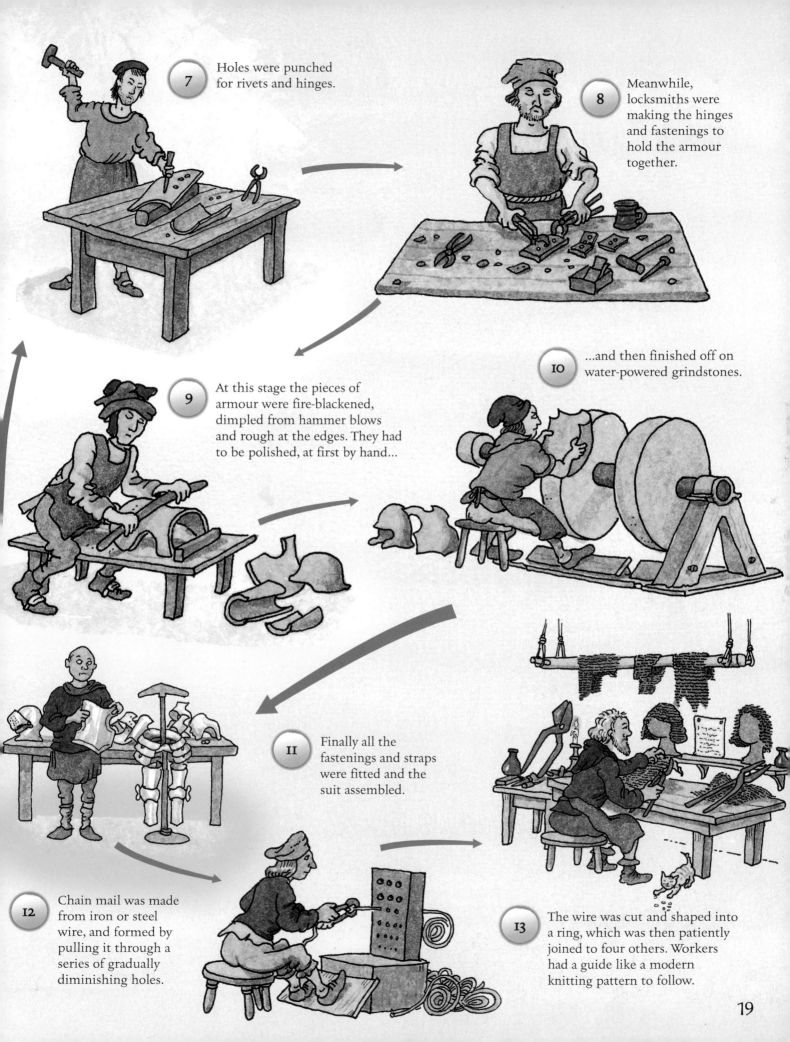

7 Holes were punched for rivets and hinges.

8 Meanwhile, locksmiths were making the hinges and fastenings to hold the armour together.

9 At this stage the pieces of armour were fire-blackened, dimpled from hammer blows and rough at the edges. They had to be polished, at first by hand...

10 ...and then finished off on water-powered grindstones.

11 Finally all the fastenings and straps were fitted and the suit assembled.

12 Chain mail was made from iron or steel wire, and formed by pulling it through a series of gradually diminishing holes.

13 The wire was cut and shaped into a ring, which was then patiently joined to four others. Workers had a guide like a modern knitting pattern to follow.

BLOODY BATTLE

Medieval battles were dreadful, muddled, bloody affairs. Once the fighting began the commanders had no control over their armies. They could not send messages and, even if they did, their soldiers would not have heard above the din of thousands of men yelling and the clanging of weapons on armour. It must have sounded like a football match in which every spectator was banging a metal bucket with a poker and shouting too.

The fighting did not last long. No man was strong and fit enough to fight for hours wearing armour and wielding a heavy weapon. Usually one army charged and there was a struggle until one side or the other turned and ran. Medieval soldiers only took prisoners who were noble and could pay a ransom to buy their freedom.

FIGHTING FOR FUN

Tournaments or mock battles were, along with hunting, the only sport of knights. They began in the 1100s as one-to-one combats and then developed into mock battles, called mêlées, that were so dangerous that many knights were killed. A safer sport was devised where two knights rode at each other, trying to unhorse one another or score points by hitting each other's shields.

A tournament was the chance for a knight to show off all his martial skills before an admiring crowd of noble ladies: the applause of common peasants was of no account even if they were allowed to watch in the first place. A tournament looked and sounded thrillingly warlike, but in reality it was no more dangerous than a game of rugby.

Asian armour

India was often invaded from the north by armies of horsemen, so cavalry (soldiers who fought on horseback) became the most important part of Indian armies. The last invaders were the Muslim Mughals who set up an empire in Delhi.

Indian soldiers wore suits of chain mail and helmets richly decorated with gold and brass. Plates of iron were added to the body and arms. Helmets were conical and pointed, like the roofs of mosques, and had adjustable nose guards. Horses and elephants were armoured, too.

Japanese warriors, or samurai, were like the medieval knights of Europe in spirit, but their armour was very different. It was lighter and more flexible than European armour, designed to absorb the shock of a blow rather than break it. A suit of armour was made of hundreds of thin strips of steel laced together with silk threads. The Japanese seemed deliberately to make their armour as complicated as possible. Each suit had dozens of parts with many different names for each of them, and there are more sorts of Japanese chain mail than from all of the rest of the world put together.

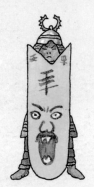

1300 CE As well as iron, Chinese armour was made from bronze, leather, wicker and even paper.

1640 Swallow-tailed shields were popular. The archer wears a leather coat studded with steel plates.

1400 Dogs and other animals carrying fire bombs were used to spread confusion amongst the enemy.

1100 The impressive armour of this heavy cavalryman and his horse is made of bronze scales.

1400 Thin strips of steel laced together were called lamellar armour. It was always light and flexible.

1600 More modern Japanese armour was made from larger steel plates, and was much less complicated.

210 BCE The figures in the Terracotta Army are exact lifesize models of ancient Chinese soldiers, such as this one.

1640 This soldier's armour is very simple and cheap. The string of bags round his neck contain rice.

JAPANESE HELMETS

Japanese helmets came in a wide range of shapes. Fierce face masks were worn to frighten the enemy as well as for protection.

23

ARMOUR IN DECLINE

As soon as handguns became widely used, armour became increasingly unpopular. It had to be made thicker to stop bullets, which made it too heavy and uncomfortable to wear. Ordinary soldiers refused to wear armour unless they were paid extra and were not made to march more than 16km a day.

It was not just guns – crossbows could also pierce armour plate – but a powerful combination of new infantry tactics and new weapons that made the knight obsolete. Swiss, German and Czech infantry learnt to fight in great squares bristling with lances, rather like the Greek phalanx. In the square were handgunners and crossbowmen who, safe amongst the spears that kept the attacking cavalry at bay, picked off the riders.

By the middle of the 16th century, armour, particularly for the infantry, was reduced to a helmet, a breastplate and a back plate with thigh protection. Men armed with muskets did not usually bother with body armour. It got in the way when they were firing, and was an extra weight to carry when added to that of their heavy gun.

1670 CE Kings and generals still wore a suit of armour for their portraits, as it made them look stern and warlike.

1848 Engineers digging trenches close to a fortress wore heavy helmets right into the 19th century.

1520 German mercenary

1560 Polish officer

1600 Pikeman

1645 A Roundhead cavalry trooper of the English Civil War.

1798 Armour finally shrank to nothing more than the small steel plate at this officer's throat.

1760 Prussian cavalry wore breast and back plates, heavy boots and a hat reinforced with iron.

1815 The armour of the French cuirassiers was not much use against cannon at the Battle of Waterloo.

1861 A few officers in the American Civil War wore steel breastplates disguised as uniform waistcoats.

25

ARMOUR MAKES A COMEBACK

In the First World War many soldiers died of head wounds, and it was soon realized that a steel helmet could save lives. The French army was the first to have them in 1915 and all other armies soon followed. Body armour was designed too, but it was too heavy to use comfortably. In the Second World War all soldiers wore helmets, but body armour was only used by bomber crews. As the men were sitting or lying down, weight was not a problem.

1918 CE German body armour was very heavy and worn only by soldiers guarding dangerous places.

1917 The loopholes in this British trench are made from steel plate and the men all wear the helmets introduced in 1916.

1939 Poison gas was used for the first time in the First World War. The first protection against it was a simple hood, but masks with air filters were later designed.

Charcoal filter

1915

WAR HELMETS

Each country had a unique and easily recognizable shape for its army's steel helmet, just as their soldiers all wore different uniforms.

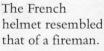

A British 'tin hat' or 'battle bowler'.

The French helmet resembled that of a fireman.

German helmets protected one's eyes and neck.

1918 Sailors wore gloves and hoods of flameproof fabric to protect them from the flash of an explosion.

1916 These Austrian messenger dogs in their hoods are safe from gas.

1917 This British body armour consisted of a metal plate inside felt lining, with padding behind.

1944 Gunners in American bombers wore a steel helmet and full body armour. Headphones in the helmet allowed communication with the pilot.

1940 This set of armour included a spade on the chest for extra protection and steel goggles.

1940 Bomb-aimers lay flat on the floor of the aircraft and often made improvised body armour from the hubcap of a car.

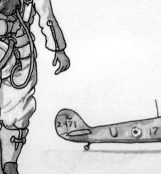

1969 Rioters in Northern Ireland threw rocks at the soldiers' unprotected ankles. They responded with armour made from baked bean tins.

Modern armour

If a knight travelled from 1400 to 1900 he would have been surprised and alarmed to see that soldiers no longer wore armour. Then, if he were to resume his time travel forward another 100 years, he would be amazed to see soldiers in armour that looked remarkably like his. Armour, made from lighter materials than steel, staged a big comeback in the late 20th century. From soldiers and police to security guards, everyone is wearing it now.

Medieval and modern soldiers look similar in their helmets and body armour – only the materials are different.

Riot police wear helmets with plastic visors, body armour and flameproof overalls. Their shields are made of clear, high-impact plastic.

Police and guards at check points carry mini-shields in the form of bullet-proof clipboards.

Even community police officers have to wear knifeproof vests made from kevlar, just in case.

American soldiers in the Vietnam War were the first in modern times to wear armour in battle.

A massive frontal plate and a helmet with a thick perspex visor protect bomb disposal officers. The suit is made of a tough, flameproof plastic fibre.

The most up-to-date armour for riot police is almost entirely made from plastic plates. It's designed to protect against stones and bottles, not bullets.

The most modern body armour is made from kevlar and ceramic plates and is fastened with velcro.

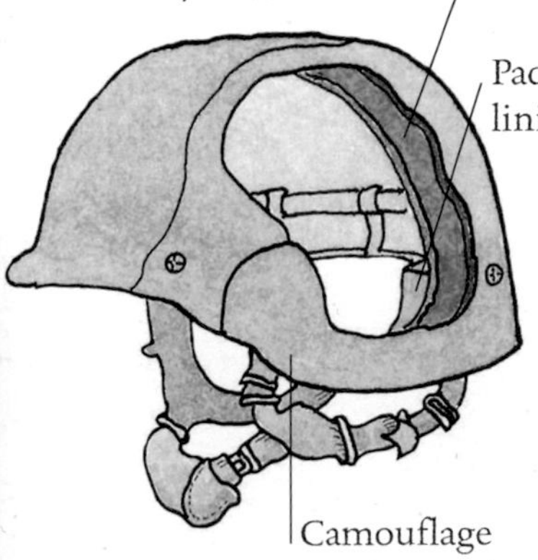

The armour of the future will be as light and easy to wear as regular clothes, but as tough as steel.

Ballistic nylon, 7mm thick

Padded lining

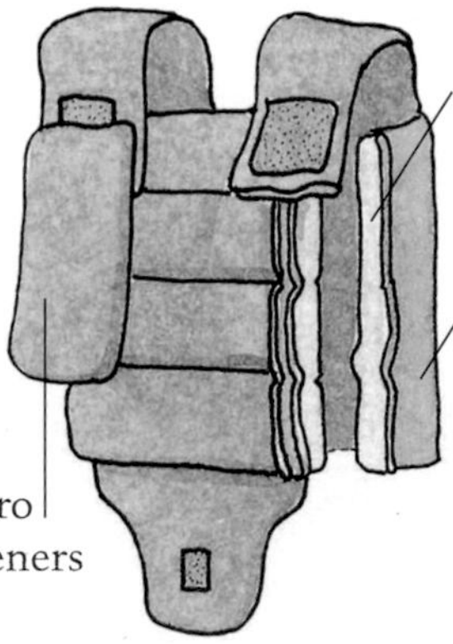

Ceramic plate

Kevlar fabric

Velcro fasteners

Camouflage coating

A modern combat helmet

Modern body armour

ATHLETIC ARMOUR

All popular sports have an element of danger, and some people love dicing with death. A game with hard balls thrown at great speed is always going to be more exciting than netball, ice hockey is more exhilarating than show jumping and it is a boring motor race that does not have at least one crash. But even the most daring athlete needs some protection...

1400 The Aztecs wore padding on their elbows and waists to play a fast and dangerous game with a solid rubber ball.

150 CE In Roman times there were many types of gladiators, each with a specific style of armour and weapons. Two similar gladiators never fought each other. The crowd liked to see two different types, pitting their individual skills against each other.

Motorcyclists wear helmets and suits of leather and kevlar with high-impact plastic inserts to protect their knees, elbows, shoulders and backs.

Fencers wear face masks of stainless steel and a jacket made of closely woven nylon.

The puck in ice hockey is hard and travels very fast. The goalkeeper is padded and protected like a medieval knight.

In the Middle Ages, hunting dogs often wore leather armour with metal studs to protect them from wild boars' tusks.

A cricket ball can travel at 175km/h, so players must wear shin pads, a helmet and thick, padded gloves.

American footballers wear helmets with face guards and elaborate body armour with shoulder pads to absorb the shocks of the game.

Football goalkeepers sometimes wear helmets. It is very dangerous diving down to grab the ball when another player is trying to kick it.

31

INDUSTRIAL ARMOUR

Industry has always been dangerous. Workers are threatened by extreme heat, poisonous fumes and falling objects. In the last 50 years, even more deadly jobs have been created. The crew of some rockets handle fuel that can dissolve them; a nuclear reactor is lethally radioactive. Specialized clothing now protects most workers in dangerous jobs. This is just as much armour as the metal suit of the knight. If there is a gap in the protection, the result is just as deadly.

Miners' helmets are made of metal, fibreglass or plastic and are usually equipped with a lamp.

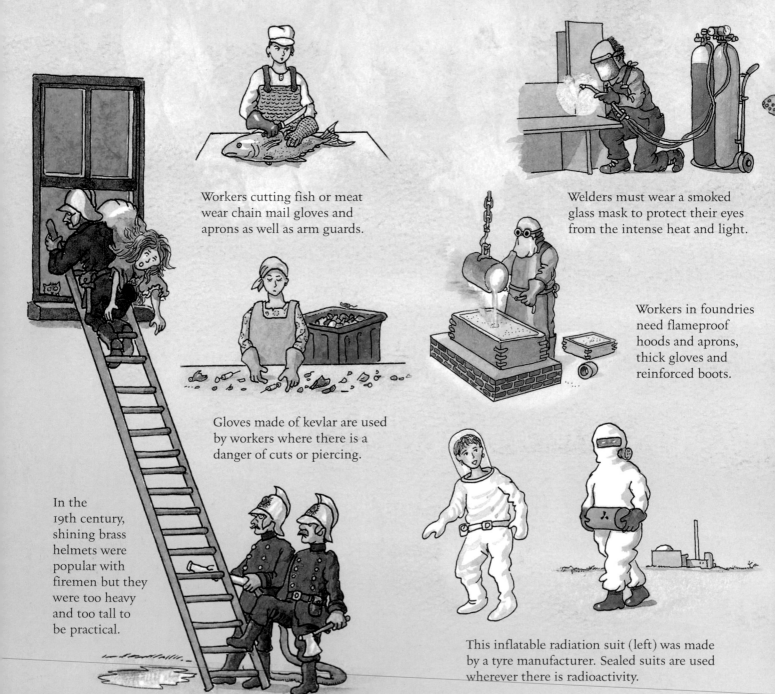

Workers cutting fish or meat wear chain mail gloves and aprons as well as arm guards.

Welders must wear a smoked glass mask to protect their eyes from the intense heat and light.

Gloves made of kevlar are used by workers where there is a danger of cuts or piercing.

Workers in foundries need flameproof hoods and aprons, thick gloves and reinforced boots.

In the 19th century, shining brass helmets were popular with firemen but they were too heavy and too tall to be practical.

This inflatable radiation suit (left) was made by a tyre manufacturer. Sealed suits are used wherever there is radioactivity.

SAFETY SUITS

Space and the depths of the sea are dangerous. In space it is extremely cold, and full of deadly cosmic rays, whizzing rocks and specks of space dust. The deep sea, too, is freezing and the pressure of the water increases with depth. To walk in space you must have a very special suit, and the only way to dive comfortably is to wear armoured diving gear. At 60m down the pressure of the water is five times greater than at the surface, so a diving suit must be very strong to resist it.

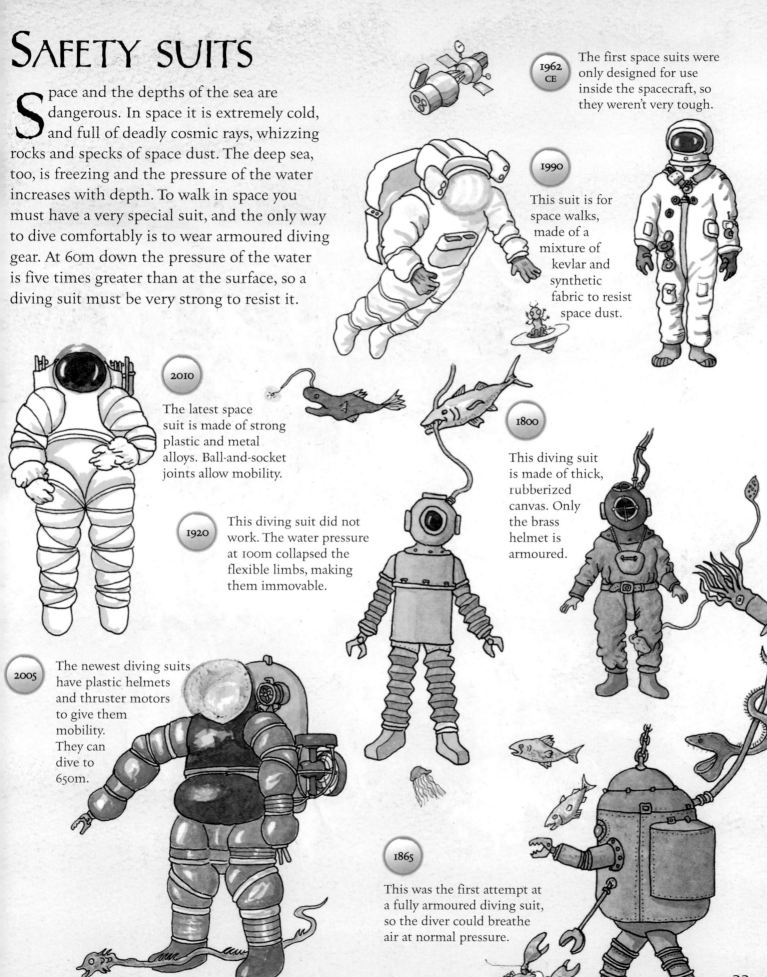

1962 CE The first space suits were only designed for use inside the spacecraft, so they weren't very tough.

1990 This suit is for space walks, made of a mixture of kevlar and synthetic fabric to resist space dust.

2010 The latest space suit is made of strong plastic and metal alloys. Ball-and-socket joints allow mobility.

1920 This diving suit did not work. The water pressure at 100m collapsed the flexible limbs, making them immovable.

1800 This diving suit is made of thick, rubberized canvas. Only the brass helmet is armoured.

2005 The newest diving suits have plastic helmets and thruster motors to give them mobility. They can dive to 650m.

1865 This was the first attempt at a fully armoured diving suit, so the diver could breathe air at normal pressure.

33

WAR WAGONS

Soldiers have dreamed of war chariots or armoured carts that could move about the battlefield since ancient times. The problem was always how to power them. Men weren't strong enough and horses pulling from outside could be killed. Horses inside took up too much room, and in any case weren't powerful enough to move a heavy vehicle over rough ground. It wasn't until the invention of small powerful engines 120 years ago that a true armoured fighting vehicle became possible.

100 CE

The Romans and the Greeks built siege towers to attack walled towns. Sometimes they were coated with plates made of iron or bronze.

900 BCE

This battering ram was used by the Assyrians to attack cities. It was protected by leather skins and the sides were made of wicker, rather like a basket.

1425

The Hussite armies in what is now the Czech Republic would draw their war carts in a circle and chain them together to make a fortress. The carts mounted many small guns and they always defeated the knights that attacked them.

1300

This was a common sight at a siege in the Middle Ages. The battering ram hung from the roof of a shed on wheels, which was protected by strong boards covered in animal hides.

c.1500 Leonardo da Vinci was a great inventor as well as an artist. He drew plans for this circular war vehicle which was powered by men turning crank handles inside. It was never built, though.

1530 If you ignore the fancy dress, this is quite a sensible siege tower. It moved forward on skids by winching itself on a pulley attached to a strong post.

1560 Guido Ramelli designed this ingenious amphibious armoured car. It was powered by four men turning the paddle wheels. When it reached dry land they changed gears to turn the four land wheels.

1580 A couple of horses inside this cart pushed it forward. But they could only have pushed it forward on firm, level ground. It couldn't cross ploughed fields.

1795 The French were about to invade England. To defend the open beaches, Captain Adam Elliott proposed a land sloop, armed with a six-pounder gun, six muskets and scythes on the wheels. It could travel at 10km/h but only if the wind was blowing!

BIRTH OF THE TANK

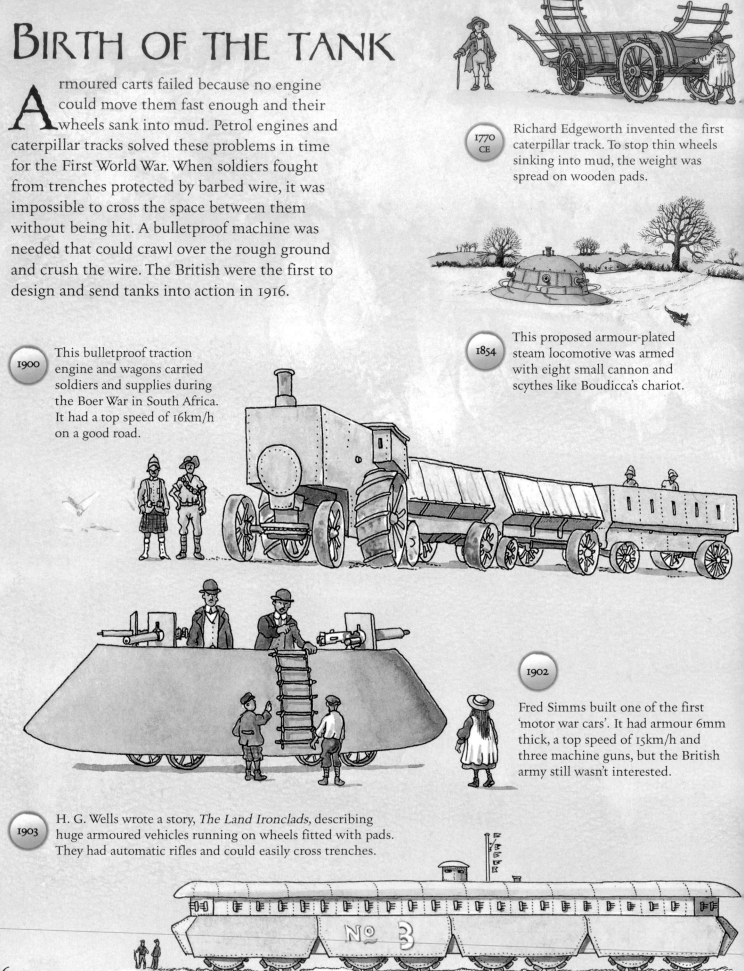

Armoured carts failed because no engine could move them fast enough and their wheels sank into mud. Petrol engines and caterpillar tracks solved these problems in time for the First World War. When soldiers fought from trenches protected by barbed wire, it was impossible to cross the space between them without being hit. A bulletproof machine was needed that could crawl over the rough ground and crush the wire. The British were the first to design and send tanks into action in 1916.

1770 CE Richard Edgeworth invented the first caterpillar track. To stop thin wheels sinking into mud, the weight was spread on wooden pads.

1854 This proposed armour-plated steam locomotive was armed with eight small cannon and scythes like Boudicca's chariot.

1900 This bulletproof traction engine and wagons carried soldiers and supplies during the Boer War in South Africa. It had a top speed of 16km/h on a good road.

1902 Fred Simms built one of the first 'motor war cars'. It had armour 6mm thick, a top speed of 15km/h and three machine guns, but the British army still wasn't interested.

1903 H. G. Wells wrote a story, *The Land Ironclads*, describing huge armoured vehicles running on wheels fitted with pads. They had automatic rifles and could easily cross trenches.

NO 3

1903 The first armoured cars were fine on good roads, but they were useless going cross-country.

1904 The Russian army was one of the first to buy an armoured car, but no more were ordered because it frightened the horses.

1914 The British army was already using tractors running on caterpillar tracks to pull heavy guns.

1915 Soon a tractor was turned into an armoured vehicle. This was the very first tank, called 'Little Willie'.

1917 Man-propelled mini-tanks seemed a good idea – on smooth ground – but the soldier's legs were dangerously exposed.

1916 The British were the first to use tanks in action. They had a gun on each side and caterpillar tracks that ran over and under the body. The spoked wheels helped them to steer.

MODERN TANKS

When British tanks first appeared, the French and Germans quickly made their own designs. They were all crude machines that now look very odd. After the war, armies experimented with different sorts of tank. Some wanted swarms of light, fast tanks, others very heavy tanks. By 1939 the classic shape of the tank had evolved, with a single turret on an armoured hull. The only difference now is that tanks have thicker armour and bigger guns.

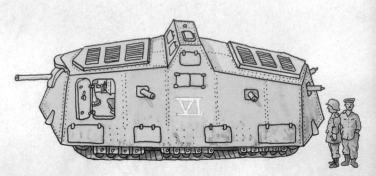

1918 CE The Germans' answer to the tank was the lumbering 32 tonne Sturmpanzerwagen with a crew of 18, six machine-guns and one small cannon. It was very slow, unable to cross ditches and so top-heavy it often fell over.

1917 France produced this clumsy tank weighing 22 tonnes and armed with a field gun and four machine guns. Its petrol/electric engine pushed it along at a crawl. It didn't fall over but got its nose stuck in ditches.

The French Renault light tank weighed only 6 tonnes and was, at 10km/h, the fastest tank of the war. It carried two men and a small cannon in a revolving turret.

1918

1930 This Mercedes was the first armoured car. The windows were protected by steel plates that sprang up when needed. The driver had a small vision slit; the passengers used a periscope.

1933 The Russians in the 1930s favoured very heavy battle tanks. The giant T-35 weighed 50 tonnes, had five turrets and a large crew of 11.

1928 Looking almost like a toy, the first British one-man tankette of 1928 was built by an army officer in his garage.

1943 The German Panther was probably the best tank of the Second World War. It was fast and heavily armoured, with a powerful gun, but was rather too complicated and often broke down.

2005 Special vans are built to carry cash and valuables. They have armoured windows, strengthened locks and can resist gunfire and ramming.

1959 In the 1950s, tracked armoured vehicles were built to ferry soldiers about the battlefield. The American M113 typically carried ten men and was armed with a single machine gun.

2010 Many police forces have special armoured vehicles armed with high pressure water cannon, that can blast rioters off their feet.

1991 The American Abrams weighs 70 tonnes but still speeds at 48km/h over rough ground. Its armour is an exotic sandwich of steel, ceramics, plastic, kevlar and depleted uranium.

ARMOURED TRAINS

Armoured trains are most useful where the distances are vast and there are few roads. In such situations the equivalent of a small battleship moving swiftly is a powerful force. They were mainly used in South Africa during the Boer War, and in Russia during the revolution and both world wars. After the Second World War they became obsolete. Armoured vehicles and helicopters can patrol more effectively, and cannot be stopped by blowing up the rails.

1864 The Union army in the American Civil War mounted a heavy gun on a railway truck behind an armoured shield. It was pushed up and down a short stretch of curved track to aim it.

1952 The British army used small petrol-engined armoured rail trolleys to patrol the railway lines in Malaysia and protect them from the attacks of rebels.

1865 A cross-section through a British armoured train designed in 1865 but never built.

1861 The first true armoured train, with a locomotive and an iron-plated wagon, was built to patrol the railway lines near Philadelphia, USA, after the Confederates had burnt several railway bridges in the American Civil War.

1920 This Russian armoured train of 1920 consists of a steam locomotive cased in bulletproof plating, and four armoured carriages armed with field guns in turrets and machine guns.

1900 Armoured trains were very useful to the British army in South Africa. This engine was boxed in steel plate and given extra protection by a curtain of thick rope. Looking like a wooly mammoth it was called 'Hairy Mary' by the soldiers.

1865 The British army thought that defending the coast with guns in armoured trains would be much cheaper than building forts and batteries, as they could be moved to wherever danger threatened.

EARLY ARMOURED SHIPS

The Romans and the Chinese sometimes put iron or brass plates on their warships, but there was no urgent need for armour until guns firing explosive shells were used in the 1840s. Shells were much more dangerous than solid cannonballs, which were usually stopped by a ship's thick timbers. The solution was to fix iron plates to the hull, and the new warships built in the second half of the 19th century became known as 'ironclads'. They were too heavy to use sail power alone and all had steam engines.

1592 The Koreans built several turtle ships to fight the Japanese. The spiked iron roof protected the crew from arrows and bullets but, most importantly, made the ship impossible to board.

1483 This fanciful floating fortress was originally drawn in 1483. The crew are armed with spears, halberds, crossbows and primitive handguns. As they are all wearing armour, they must be very confident that the ship will not be sunk.

1859 France launched the first seagoing armoured ship in 1859: the *Gloire*. She was 78m long and weighed 5,630 tonnes. Her armour was 121mm thick and she was armed with 36 guns.

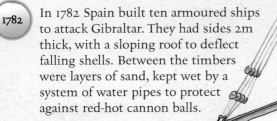

1782 In 1782 Spain built ten armoured ships to attack Gibraltar. They had sides 2m thick, with a sloping roof to deflect falling shells. Between the timbers were layers of sand, kept wet by a system of water pipes to protect against red-hot cannon balls.

1860 Not to be outdone by France, Britain built HMS *Warrior*, which was much bigger and faster than the *Gloire*. At 128m long, weighing 9,137 tonnes with iron armour 114mm thick, she carried 40 guns. Beautifully restored, HMS *Warrior* is moored at Portsmouth in the UK and is well worth a visit.

BATTLE OF THE IRONCLADS: USS MONITOR v CSS VIRGINIA

When the American Civil War began, the Union navy blockaded the Confederate coast to stop them getting supplies. The Confederates decided to build an armoured ship to destroy the wooden Union ships. They took the hull of a frigate, renamed her *Virginia*, and cut the sides down to within half a metre of the water. On the deck they built a casemate (an armoured enclosure for guns) with thick, sloping wooden sides covered with iron plates.

The next day, the *Virginia* sailed out to finish off the rest of the Union fleet only to be met by another, even weirder ship. Looking like 'a cheese box on a plank', the USS *Monitor* was truly revolutionary: the first ship to mount guns in a revolving turret. The historic first battle between armoured ships lasted four hours. *Virginia* was hit 41 times and *Monitor* 21, but neither could injure the other. The fight was a draw, but the overall battle was a victory for the *Monitor* because she saved the rest of the fleet.

On 7 March 1862 the *Virginia* steamed into the estuary of Hampton Roads. The Union ships fired furiously, but their shot and shell bounced off the *Virginia* as she slowly advanced to sink two warships and force another aground.

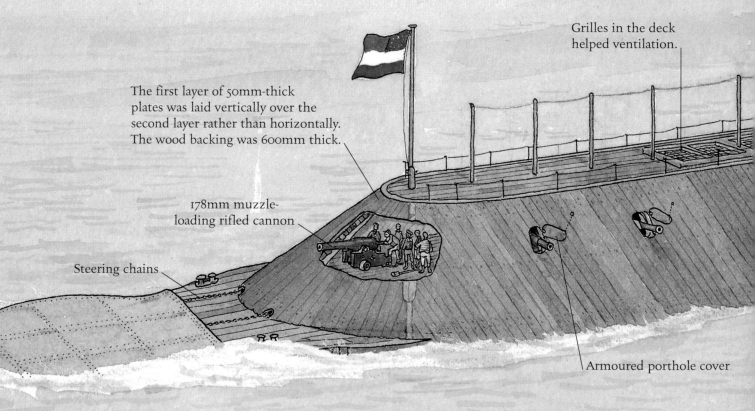

Grilles in the deck helped ventilation.

The first layer of 50mm-thick plates was laid vertically over the second layer rather than horizontally. The wood backing was 600mm thick.

178mm muzzle-loading rifled cannon

Steering chains

Armoured porthole cover

The engines of the *Virginia* were always breaking down and she could only steam at a speed of 6km/h. Her armour was 100mm thick and made from railway tracks that had been heated and rolled into plates.

Only the armoured casemate of the *Virginia* showed above the water. It mounted ten guns. A ram was fitted to the bows but it broke off in the first attack.

The *Monitor* was designed by a Swedish engineer, John Ericsson, and took only three months to build. She weighed 1,225 tonnes and was made entirely of iron.

The graceful, wooden steam frigate USS *Merrimack* was cut down a deck and turned into the *Virginia*, like a swan into an ugly duckling.

Conning tower

Coal bunker

Boilers

Conning tower made of iron logs 230mm thick.

The *Monitor*'s turret was turned by a steam engine. Its walls were 203mm thick and inside were two 280mm smooth bore guns firing 80kg shot. The grille in the roof let smoke escape.

45

MODERN BATTLESHIPS

The first ironclads mounted their guns in rows along the sides or in turrets. It was not obvious which was best. The rest of the 19th century was a time of experimentation, and many odd designs were tried out until the turret was accepted. Although all battleships were powered by steam, most carried sails until the 1890s. The classic modern battleship of the last century carried enormous guns in three or four turrets, with armour up to 400mm thick.

0   50m

1865 The turret ship *Huascar* was built in Britain for Peru. She was captured by Chile in 1879 and still survives as a museum ship.

1867 The German *Kronprinz* was a typical broadside ironclad of the 1860s, with sails and a ram bow. She had armour 127mm thick and carried 16 guns.

1872

The Royal Navy's *Thunderer* was the first battleship without sails. She carried four 305mm guns in two turrets. There was a terrible accident aboard when a gun was loaded twice by mistake and exploded.

0   50m

0   50m

1944 USS *Missouri*, 1944, was the fastest ever battleship with a speed of 61km/h. She carried nine 406mm guns and last saw action in the Gulf War of 1991 before retiring the following year.

0   50m

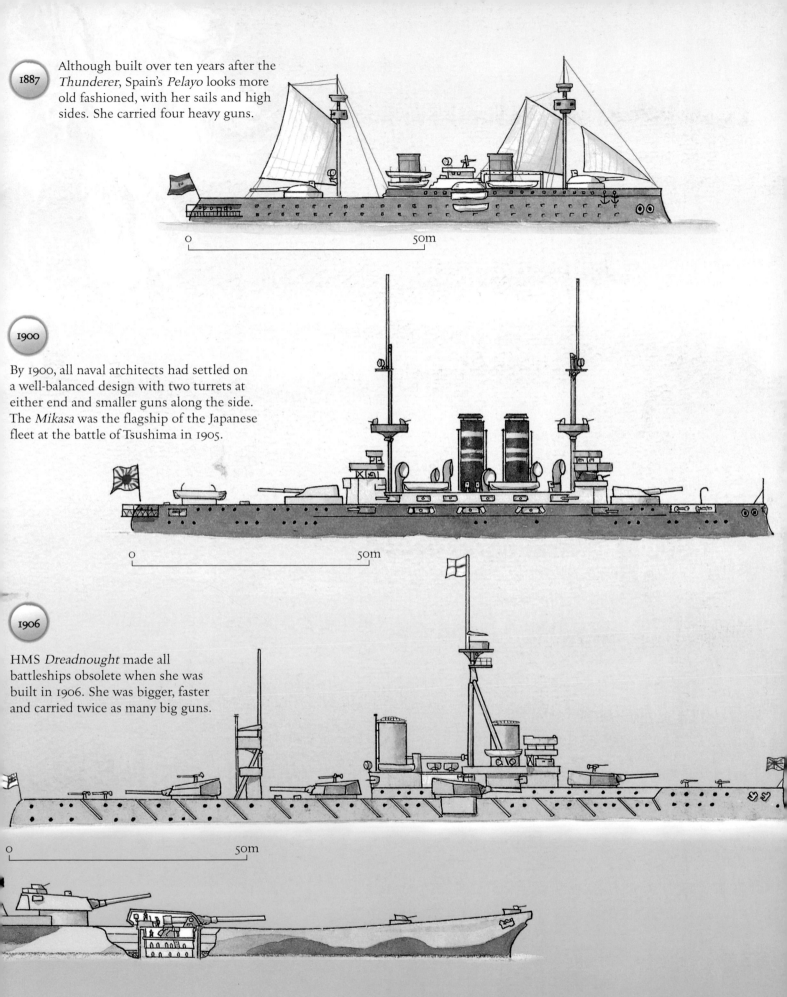

1887 Although built over ten years after the *Thunderer*, Spain's *Pelayo* looks more old fashioned, with her sails and high sides. She carried four heavy guns.

o   50m

1900 By 1900, all naval architects had settled on a well-balanced design with two turrets at either end and smaller guns along the side. The *Mikasa* was the flagship of the Japanese fleet at the battle of Tsushima in 1905.

o   50m

1906 HMS *Dreadnought* made all battleships obsolete when she was built in 1906. She was bigger, faster and carried twice as many big guns.

o   50m

DEEP-SEA DIVING VESSELS

Some of the most heavily armoured ships are not protected against the sudden blow of a shell but from the slow, steady, terrible crushing pressure of the depths of the sea. Water is very heavy, and the deeper an object sinks the greater the pressure on it. Thousands of metres down, tonnes press on every square centimetre. A vessel designed to explore the still-mysterious ocean deeps has to be immensely strong.

Thruster

Ballast spheres

Batteries

The very latest deep-diving craft are designed to be very mobile, 'flying' through the water on stubby wings. The cockpit is made of very tough plastic – strong enough to resist the pressure at 300m.

Entrance tower

Propellers

Stabilizing fin

Ballast of iron shot

Entrance tube

Crew compartment

Buoyancy tank of gasoline

Auguste Piccard designed *Trieste*, a bathyscaphe (Greek for 'deep ship') that floated, rising to the surface without the need for a heavy cable, and with propellers so it could move.

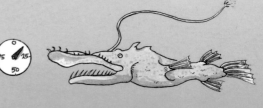

A submarine is safe as long as it doesn't go below its designated safe depth. That depth depends on the strength of the hull.

As the submarine sinks deeper the pressure increases and, once beyond the safe limit, something will give way and water will cascade in. But once the submarine is full of water, the pressure will equalize and, however deep it sinks, it will not be squashed any further.

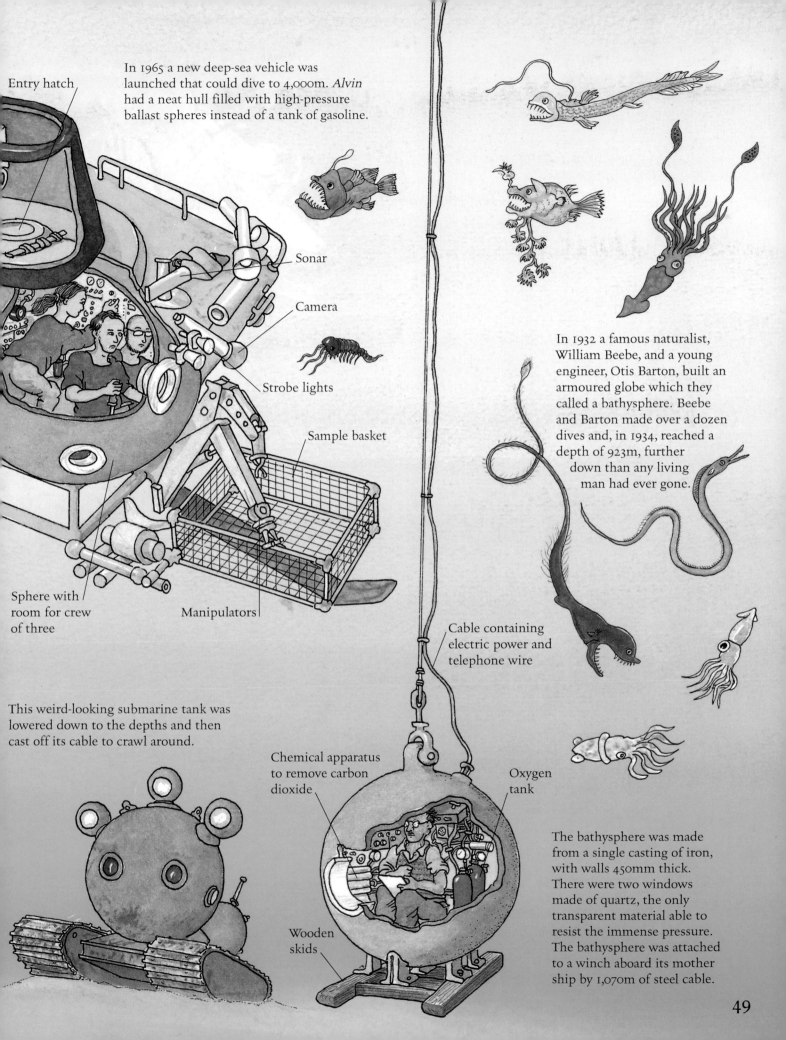

Entry hatch

In 1965 a new deep-sea vehicle was launched that could dive to 4,000m. *Alvin* had a neat hull filled with high-pressure ballast spheres instead of a tank of gasoline.

Sonar

Camera

Strobe lights

Sample basket

Manipulators

Sphere with room for crew of three

In 1932 a famous naturalist, William Beebe, and a young engineer, Otis Barton, built an armoured globe which they called a bathysphere. Beebe and Barton made over a dozen dives and, in 1934, reached a depth of 923m, further down than any living man had ever gone.

Cable containing electric power and telephone wire

This weird-looking submarine tank was lowered down to the depths and then cast off its cable to crawl around.

Chemical apparatus to remove carbon dioxide

Oxygen tank

Wooden skids

The bathysphere was made from a single casting of iron, with walls 450mm thick. There were two windows made of quartz, the only transparent material able to resist the immense pressure. The bathysphere was attached to a winch aboard its mother ship by 1,070m of steel cable.

49

ARMOURED PLANES

During the First World War, aircraft started flying low to attack targets on the ground. Many were shot down, so designers produced rugged metal planes fitted with armour. Many Second World War fighters had armour around the cockpit and bombers had armoured seats for the pilots. Today, jets fly so fast that armour is unnecessary except for ground attack aircraft. The danger to passenger planes is more often from inside. Flight deck doors have strong locks and strengthened luggage containers lessen the damage caused by a bomb smuggled into a suitcase.

1974

The A-10 Thunderbolt was designed to fight Russian tanks. It has a 30mm anti-tank gun in the nose and the pilot sits in a bath of thick, light and tough titanium armour.

1918

The German Junkers J-4 was the first all-metal biplane. The crew, engine and petrol tank were all protected by sheets of 5mm armour.

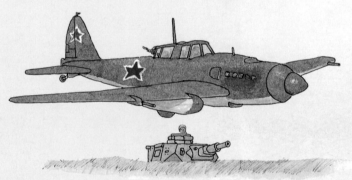

1941

The Russian Stormovik's nickname was 'The Flying Tank' because it was so heavily armoured. They flew close to the ground and destroyed thousands of German vehicles in the Second World War.

2010

Attack and troop-carrying helicopters have to fly low and slowly over the battlefield, so they are protected around the cockpit and engine with lightweight plastic and ceramic armour.

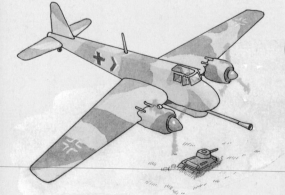

1942

The windscreen of the German Henschel Hs 129 was 75mm thick, and the cockpit was armour-plated. Its huge 75mm gun was deadly to Russian tanks.

1884 Only the cabin of this proposed steam-powered airship was armoured. It would have been impossible to protect the gas bag, but without armour a single shot could have brought it down.

1981 The space shuttle is armoured with ceramic tiles on its underside, nose and wing edges. The tiles protect it against the fierce heat caused by friction on entering the earth's atmosphere.

ARMOURED BUILDINGS

Doors and windows are the weakest point in any building. Since early times doors have been strengthened with bolts, and windows covered by bars. In modern cities many homes and offices have security grilles over their doors and windows. Some have armoured shutters and even bulletproof windows. The Oval Office of the US president has windows able to withstand a small missile.

This medieval door has its thick timbers bound with iron straps. A tiny barred window allows the doorkeeper to see who's knocking.

In warm countries, downstairs windows were covered by iron grilles so the house could be open to the air but not robbers or, in this picture, would-be suitors.

The strongest and heaviest doors are found in bank vaults, safes and strong rooms. Designed to resist attack by explosives and heat cutters, they have very complicated locks.

The 'Impregnable Iron Fortress', designed in England in 1860, had walls of iron blocks dovetailed together with portholes for 70 cannon. Three were proposed to guard the Thames estuary but were never built.

Some German forts were built with walls made from large iron plates. These were assembled like giant pieces of flat-pack furniture.

This Russian fort was built in 1897 to protect the entrance to Saint Petersburg harbour. The front wall is made of iron plate.

In 1940 Britain feared invasion by the German army from across the English Channel, and thousands of concrete pillboxes and gun batteries were quickly built. A cheap alternative was this small steel turret. Its machine gun could fire from the roof against aircraft or from the front against troops and tanks.

In the Second World War, railway workers and sentries were often caught out in an air-raid and needed to find shelter quickly. Steel one-man shelters like this were quick and simple to install and could be moved easily. Anyone inside was safe from everything except a direct hit.

Fort Copacabana was built in 1914 to defend the entrance to Rio de Janeiro harbour, Brazil. All that can be seen is the concrete roof and the two gun turrets.

Iron Island

This extraordinary iron fort sits in the sea a couple of kilometres away from Portsmouth, in England. It cost a fortune, took nearly 20 years to finish and never fired its guns at an enemy. So why was it built?

More than 150 years ago, cannon had a very short range. They could not hit anything much more than a kilometre away. This was a big problem for the army, who wanted to defend the approach to Portsmouth, which was Britain's most important naval base.

It was nearly 6.5km from Portsmouth across the stretch of water called the Solent to the Isle of Wight. Any ship sailing down the middle of the Solent would be quite safe; no gun on land could hit it. If only there was another island in the Solent, dreamed the army. Then, ingenious Victorian engineers solved the problem and built artificial islands in the sea with a fort on each. Work started in 1861.

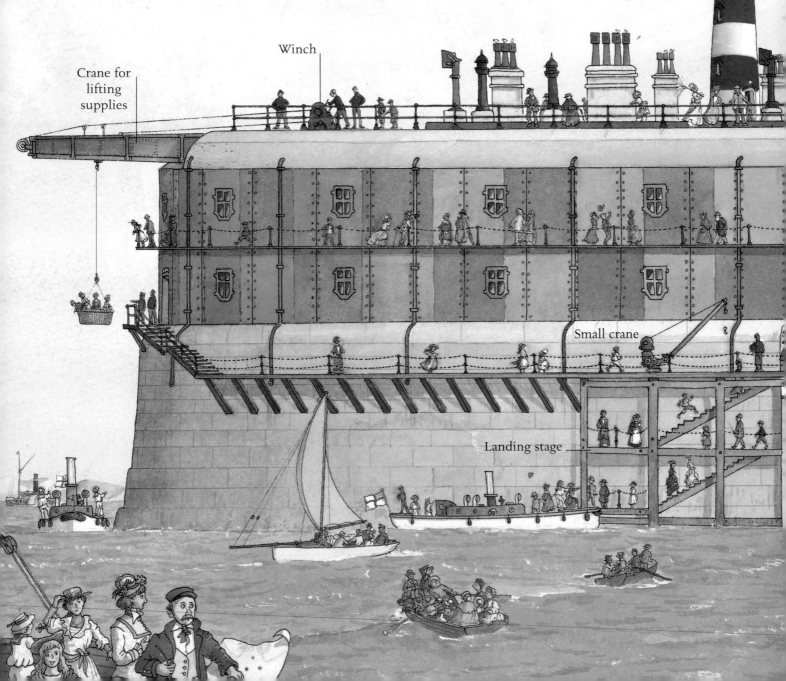

Crane for lifting supplies

Winch

Small crane

Landing stage

The biggest of the forts was called No Man's Land. It was completely circular and armed with 49 heavy guns. The bottom floors were made of hard granite, but the top two storeys were built of iron. The outside wall was a sandwich of armour plate and especially hard iron concrete 400mm thick. The fort's skin weighed 2,500 tonnes, probably the heaviest suit of armour ever made. And probably the most expensive: the fort cost the enormous sum (in those days) of around half a million pounds.

It was painted in a chequered pattern of black and yellow squares, with a lighthouse on top to warn ships. The fort had its own bakery and fresh water from a well. The garrison of 300 soldiers exercised by running around the roof, swimming and hauling the heavy shells to the guns.

But almost as soon as the fort was finished, new guns were invented that could fire up to 16km, and No Man's Land was rendered useless.

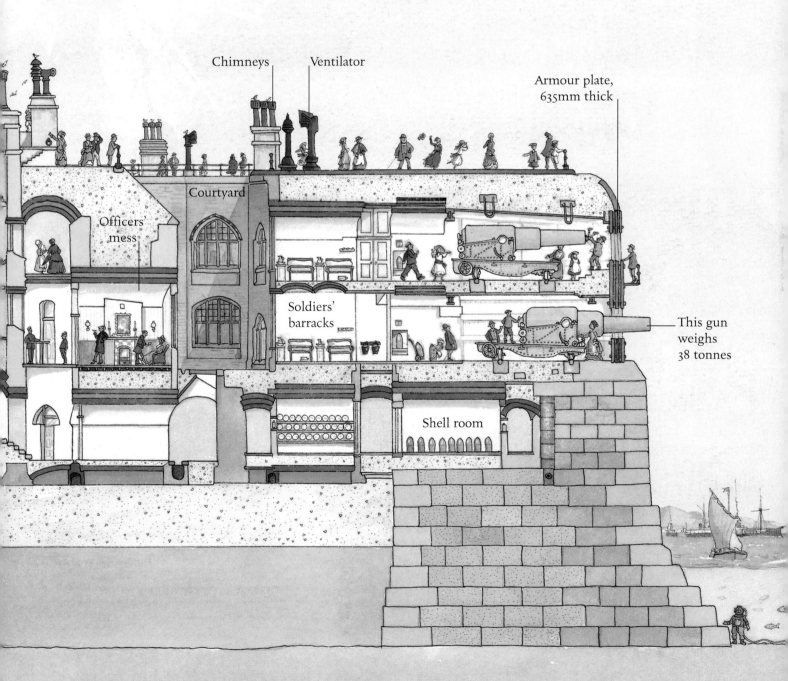

Chimneys

Ventilator

Armour plate, 635mm thick

Courtyard

Officers' mess

Soldiers' barracks

This gun weighs 38 tonnes

Shell room

Forts on land

In the late 19th century, guns firing high explosive shells forced a redesign of all forts on land. The new underground forts were made of concrete and covered with earth. All the guns were in armoured turrets that could fire in any direction, so a fort needed fewer guns to cover the same area and the guns were completely protected. All that could be seen from a distance was a low mound with a few metal domes showing above the grass.

In the 1930s, the French built a chain of forts called the Maginot Line to defend the border with Germany. All that was visible above ground were gun turrets that popped up to fire, and steel lookout and machine gun turrets like this. Underneath was virtually a small town, with stores, barracks, a power station and even an underground railway.

Switzerland had many forts with armoured turrets in the Alps, guarding roads and railway lines until the 1990s. They were often disguised in ingenious ways. Inside this cowshed is a turret with a heavy gun.

During the Second World War, the Japanese used small steel pillboxes to defend islands in the Pacific. They were light enough to be moved to wherever they were needed.

These mobile armoured turrets were used in the fortifications of Romania. The wheels were only used to move them to a prepared position.

When the Germans occupied the French city of Strasbourg in 1871, they strengthened its fortifications. Small iron forts called *caponiers* were sited in front of the ramparts to give covering fire in case an enemy crossed the ditch. Each had four small cannon.

Before the First World War the Germans secretly built a battery of giant guns powerful enough to destroy any fort in the world. Each gun weighed 75 tonnes and fired a 930kg shell.

The damage done by the giant German guns was terrible. Steel turrets were cracked like eggs and thick concrete roofs smashed open.

Observation turret

Gun turrets

Unclimbable steel fence

Machine guns to fire along the ditch

Barbed wire

Main gate

Ammunition store

At the start of the First World War there were hundreds of forts like this all over Europe. A typical fortified city, like Liege in Belgium, was surrounded by a dozen or more forts at intervals of a couple of kilometres.

Ditch

Magic armour

Every warrior's dream was for some magic defence; an invisible layer that would deflect arrows and sword cuts and make him invulnerable. That sort of magic only exists in legends of gods and heroes, but soldiers have always gone into battle hoping to be kept safe by heavenly means as well as earthly. Spells and prayers have always been recited over armour to give it extra strength and, even today, priests sprinkle modern battle tanks with holy water.

Most armour was blessed in the Middle Ages. Some armour had a holy relic fixed to it in the pious hope that the saints would make extra efforts to protect the wearer.

When Achilles, the Greek hero of the Trojan Wars, was a baby, his mother dipped him into the magic waters of the River Styx so that no weapon could ever harm him. Unfortunately she forgot about his heel, which she held as she dunked him. It was here that he was later hit by an arrow and killed.

Some Celtic warriors fought naked to show how brave they were. They painted their bodies with blue woad in magic patterns, in the belief that this would protect them.

Native American warriors who had taken part in a special religious ceremony – the Ghost Dance – wore a buckskin shirt decorated with magic symbols. Unfortunately it was no use at all against the bullets of the US cavalry.

Dervishes, the followers of the Mahdi (a spiritual leader) in the Sudan, wore quilted cotton robes called *jibbahs*. They believed the special cotton patches and their faith would keep them safe from bullets. They were wrong.

PRIVATE ARMOUR

Armour is not just for soldiers. Anybody who feels in danger wants to be protected, but steel armour is too heavy and can't be worn with ordinary clothes. Bulletproof vests made out of silk and cotton were developed in the late 1800s and were surprisingly effective. Politicians and royalty who feared assassination were eager to buy them.

John Bradshaw, the judge at King Charles I of England's trial, was so frightened of being shot by an angry royalist that he wore a hat reinforced with iron and a breastplate under his robes.

Ned Kelly and his gang of Australian bandits wore suits of armour made from plough blades. They were bulletproof but did not cover the legs, so that was where the police shot Kelly.

The 1920s were a violent time in some American cities. Gangsters and private detectives were the best customers for bulletproof vests.

These stylish steel spectacles were on sale at the beginning of the Second World War.

As the threat of war loomed in 1938, this armoured gas-proof pram went on sale. Very few were bought because, unsurprisingly, nobody wanted to take their baby out in an air-raid.

Mums worried by the threat of drive-by shootings on the mean streets of the USA can keep their baby safe in this armoured buggy, guaranteed proof against machine gun bullets.

GLOSSARY

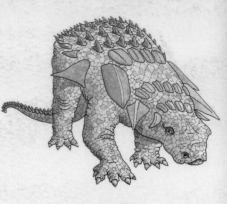

amphibious Having the ability to move equally well on land and water. Amphibious vehicles have been around since the 16th century.

Assyria A fierce and warlike power that dominated the Middle East from 900–600BCE.

ball and socket joint A flexible joint formed by one part ending in a ball and the other in a curved socket to hold the ball. A natural version of this is where the leg joins the hip.

brass A metal made from mixing copper with zinc. Copper is a very soft metal and zinc makes it harder.

breech-loading Loading a gun from the breech, or opposite end from the muzzle. This method is easier, faster and safer than muzzle-loading.

bronze A metal made from copper and tin.

cast iron When iron melts, it can be formed or cast into almost any shape by being poured into a mould.

ceramic A material made from non-metallic elements by the application of heat, such as a tile, a brick or a pot. Ceramic plates can be very strong and are lighter than metal ones.

Confederate In 1861, the 11 southern states of the USA split from the northern states to form their own country, which they called the Confederate States of America. This led to a civil war between the Confederates and the remaining states, who were known as the Federals, or the Union. The Confederates were defeated in 1865 and rejoined the USA.

cuirass Armour protecting the upper body, consisting of a breast and back plate.

cuirassier A cavalryman wearing a cuirass and helmet.

cupola A small, rounded dome on a fort used either for observation or to protect guns.

Dayak A group of tribes who live by the rivers in Borneo and Sarawak, in Malaysia. They used to be famous for headhunting.

depleted uranium A very dense metal – almost twice as heavy as lead – that is used to make armour and bullets.

fibreglass A metal made from glass spun into fine threads. Mixed with plastic resin, it makes a strong material that is easily moulded into shape.

gauntlet A heavy glove of leather or steel.

halberd A fearsome weapon with a combined axe blade, spear and hook mounted on the end of a long pole.

Hittite An appropriate name for the fierce and warlike people who were the dominant power in what is now Turkey from 1750–1200BCE.

Hussites The followers of the religious leader Jan Huss (c.1369–1415) in what is now the Czech Republic. They wanted their own national church and fought for many years against the armies of the German Emperor, who wanted to make them part of the Roman Catholic Church.

ironclad The first armoured ships were actually wooden ships with an outer layer of iron plate, hence the name 'ironclad'. Later all armoured ship were called ironclads even though they were built of, and armoured with, steel.

kevlar A very strong synthetic material made from spun plastic fibres. It is woven into sheets to make modern body armour and protective clothing.

loophole A narrow slit window in a castle or fort from which bows or guns are fired.

muzzle The dangerous end of a gun from which the bullet emerges.

muzzle-loading A cannon that is loaded from the end of the muzzle. This is always a slower process than breech-loading.

pike A very long spear.

red-hot shot Solid cannon balls heated in a furnace then fired at wooden ships to set them ablaze.

rifled cannon A cannon with twisting grooves cut inside the barrel. These spin the shell as it is fired to make it go further and with greater accuracy.

rubberized Describes materials such as cloth or canvas that have been treated with a rubber solution to make them waterproof.

shell A projectile filled with explosive. At first they were round like solid cannon balls, but those fired from rifled cannon were cylinders with a pointed end.

sloop A small sailing ship with a single mast.

smooth bore A cannon with no grooves inside the barrel.

sonar SOund Navigation And Ranging – a machine that sends out sound waves to measure the depth of water or detect obstacles and other vessels.

steel An alloy or mixture of mainly iron, with a tiny amount of carbon to add strength. It is much stronger and more flexible than pure iron.

strobe A very bright light flashing at a regular frequency, e.g. 50 times a second.

Sumerian Sumer was the first civilization where people lived in cities. It flourished in Mesopotamia or what is now modern Iraq from about 3000–1900BCE.

synthetic An artificial material made by putting together separate elements. Rubber is a natural material produced by trees, but synthetic rubber can be made from chemicals.

titanium A metal that is much stronger than steel but weighs only half as much.

Union During the American Civil War the northern states were known as the Union, as they were still part of the United States of America.

visor The moveable part of a helmet covering the face.

wrought iron Iron is wrought when hammered into shape while red hot – think of a blacksmith shaping a horseshoe – rather than melted and poured into a mould.

FURTHER INFORMATION

Where to see armour

Many museums have small collections of armour or the odd piece, but those listed here are some of the very best, with beautiful examples of the armourers' skill. Many museums hold regular events with mock fights and tournaments, and some even let you try on the armour.

Austria
The Armoury of the State of Styria, Graz (www.zeughaus.at)
Art History Museum, Vienna (www.khm.at)

Belgium
Army and Military History Museum, Brussels (www.klm-mra.be)

Canada
The Royal Ontario Museum, Toronto (http://images.rom.on.ca/public/index.php?function=browse&action=selected&tbl=aa&filter=aa_cat&fid=1&sid=&ccid=)

Denmark
The Royal Arsenal Museum, Copenhagen (www.thm.dk)

France
Army Museum, Les Invalides, Paris (www.invalides.org)

Germany
The Baden State Museum, Karlsruhe (www.landesmuseum.de/website)
The Bavarian National Museum, Munich (www.bayerisches-nationalmuseum.de)
The Bavarian Army Museum, Ingoldstadt (www.bayerisches-armeemuseum.de)
The Imperial Castle, Nuremberg (www.schloesser.bayern.de/englisch/palace/objects/nbg_burg.htm)

Italy
Churburg Castle, Churburg (www.churburg.com/willkommen_engl/index.html)
Bargello, Florence (www.polomuseale.firenze.it/english/musei/bargello)
Royal Armoury, Turin (www.artito.arti.beniculturali.it/Armeria%20Reale/DefaultArmeria.htm)

Japan
National Museum, Tokyo (www.tnm.go.jp)

The Netherlands
Army Museum, Delft (www.armymuseum.nl)

Russia
Kremlin Museum, Moscow (www.kreml.ru/en/main/museums/)
State Hermitage Museum, St Petersburg (www.hermitagemuseum.org)

Spain
Royal Armoury, Madrid (www.patrimonionacional.es/Home/Palacios-Reales/Palacio-Real-de-Madrid.aspx)

Sweden
The Royal Armoury, Stockholm (www.livrustkammaren.se)

Switzerland
National Museum, Zurich (www.musee-suisse.com)
Museum of History, Berne (www.bhm.ch)

UK
Fitzwilliam Museum, Cambridge (www.fitzmuseum.cam.ac.uk)
Art Gallery and Museum, Glasgow (www.glasgowmuseums.com)
Royal Armouries, Leeds (www.royalarmouries.org)
British Museum, London (www.britishmuseum.org/default.aspx)
National Army Museum, London (www.national-army-museum.ac.uk)
Tower of London, London (www.hrp.org.uk/TowerOfLondon)
The Wallace Collection, London (www.wallacecollection.org)
Victoria and Albert Museum, London (www.vam.ac.uk)
Warwick Castle, Warwick (www.warwick-castle.co.uk)

USA
The Art Institute of Chicago, Chicago (www.artic.edu/aic)
Museum of Art, Cleveland (www.clemusart.com)
Metropolitan Museum of Art, New York (www.metmuseum.org)
The Higgins Armory Museum, Worcester (www.higgins.org)

Where to see armoured ships

From 1860 to 1944, hundreds of armoured warships were built but hardly more than a dozen have been preserved. The USA has the most, but Britain has the oldest, HMS *Warrior*, still afloat at Portsmouth.

Chile
Huascar (1865), Talcahuano (www.oz.net/markhow/pre-dred/huascar.htm)

Greece
Georgios Averoff (1910), Faliron, Athens (www.bsaverof.com)

Japan
HIJMS *Mikasa* (1902), Yokosuka
(www.midwaysailor.com/mikasa/index.html)

The Netherlands
HNLMS *Schorpioen* (1868), The Dutch Navy Museum, Den Helder
(www.hnsa.org/ships/schorpioen.htm)
HNMLS *Buffel* (1868), Maritime Museum, Rotterdam
(www.hnsa.org/ships/buffel.htm)

UK
HMS *Warrior* (1860), Portsmouth (www.hmswarrior.org)

USA
USS *Olympia* (1895), Independence Seaport Museum, Philadelphia
(www.phillyseaport.org/ships_olympia.shtml)
USS *Texas* (1910), Houston, Texas (www.usstexasbb35.com)
USS *North Carolina* (1940), Wilmington, North Carolina
(www.battleshipnc.com)
USS *Massachusetts* (1942), Fall River, Massachusetts
(www.battleshipcove.org)
USS *Alabama* (1942), Mobile, Alabama (www.ussalabama.com)
USS *New Jersey* (1942), Camden, New Jersey
(www.battleshipnewjersey.org)
USS *Missouri* (1944), Pearl Harbor, Hawaii (www.ussmissouri.com)

Where to see tanks

Austria
Museum of Military History, Vienna (www.hgm.or.at/eng)

France
Museum of Armoured Vehicles, Saumur (www.museedesblindes.fr)

Germany
German Tank Museum, Munster (www.germantankmuseum.de)

Israel
Israeli Tank Museum, Latrun (www.yadlashiryon.com)

Russia
Kubinka Tank Museum, Moscow
(www.kubinka.ru/newindex.php?id=3&lang=2)

UK
Bovington Tank Museum, Dorset (www.tankmuseum.org)
The Imperial War Museum, London (http://london.iwm.org.uk)

USA
US Army Ordnance Museum, Aberdeen Proving Ground, Maryland
(www.peachmountain.com/5star/US_Army_Ordnance_Museum.aspx)

Where to see armoured trains
Finland
The Armour Museum, Parola (www.panssarimuseo.fi/nayttelyt.html)

Russia
Kubinka Tank Museum, Moscow (www.tankmuseum.ru/train4.html)

Where to see armoured forts
Belgium
Fort Loncin, Liege (www.palmerstonforts.org.uk/gall/loncin.php)
Fort Eben-Emael, near Maastricht (www.fort-eben-emael.be/home.php)

Brazil
Fort Copacabana, Rio de Janeiro (www.fortedecopacabana.com)

Finland
Fort Kuivasaari, Helsinki (www.nortfort.ru/coastal/foto_kvs3_e.html)

France
Fort de Fermont, near Longwy (www.ligne-maginot-fort-de-fermont.asso.fr/)
Fort du Hackenberg, near Thionville (www.maginot-hackenberg.com)

Italy
Fort Montecchio, Colic, Lake Como (www.fortemontecchionord.it)

Switzerland
Fort Verein-Magletsch, Oberschan (www.afom.ch)
Fort Airolo, St Gotthard (www.unterirdischeschweiz.ch/100015.html)

INDEX

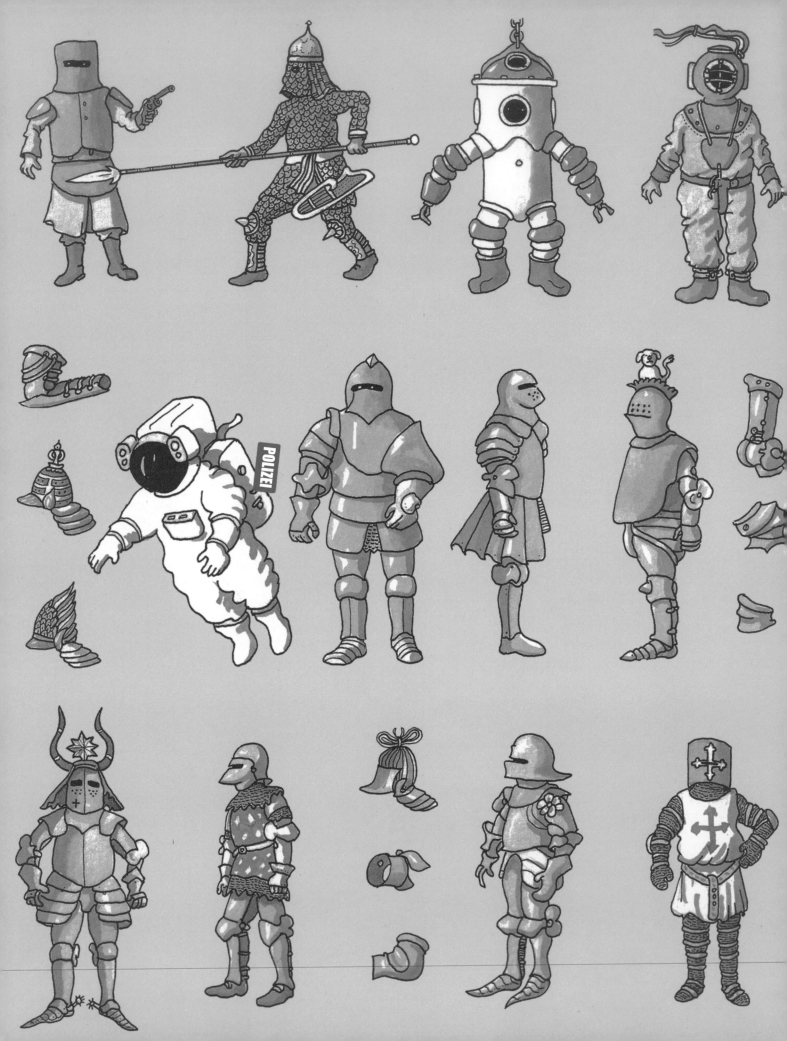